# STAY SAFE!
## A Science Fiction Play

Ian August

# Uproar Theatrics

**LICENSING & PRODUCTION INQUIRIES**
**Uproar Theatrics, LLC.**
**hello@uproartheatrics.com | www.UproarTheatrics.com**

# CAST OF CHARACTERS:

The Denizens (Clockwise, starting from USC)
BINS – Custodial
FLORA – Sustenance
STEWARD – Security
TAILOR – Textiles
GYM – Physical Training
WRENCH – Mechanics
TAB – Medic
DEETS – Historian
ASTRID STARPEPPER – Virtual SuperGuide
MAN

*Location:*
The multiple rooms of the DISC, the Denizen Isolation Security Compound, a facility designed to contain and protect the most vulnerable from one of the world's deadliest nuclear disasters.

*Time:*
The not-so-distant future; perhaps somewhere in the 2050s

*Notes on Casting:*
Aside from MAN and ASTRID STARPEPPER, the genders of all the characters are interchangeable. Simply adjust the pronouns being used in the script to match the gender identity of the actors involved.

If the role of WRENCH is played by a female identifying actor, the name "ELIAS" can be changed to "ELISA;" The references to a "son" can be changed to "daughter, " etc. Other names (page 57/58) can be altered to suit the gender breakdown of the cast at the discretion of the company.

The ensemble of this play should be portrayed by actors of various abilities, ethnicities, and gender identities. Diversity is key to the success of this piece—please find a way to make your company as diverse as possible.

*Notes on the World of the Play:*
The Denizens communicate via a video screen in each room that connects to each of the other rooms. These screens are located over the audience, literally on the fourth wall. The system is referred to as the VizCom. The VizCom is also used to communicate information throughout the facility from the Virtual Superguides, including various forms of instruction, morning, afternoon, and evening greetings, and essential communiqués.

Items are transported between rooms in the D.I.S.C. using a robotic transportation system known as JOHNNY ROCKETS, a robot maintained entirely by Wrench. JOHNNY ROCKETS can be a remote-controlled object (maybe a modified train that travels in a perpetual loop?), an additional performer, or a puppet manipulated by an actor in black. When in sleep mode, JOHNNY ROCKETS resides just outside Wrench's door, facing away from the audience. It is important that JOHNNY ROCKETS, however manifested, be adorable AF.

*STAY SAFE!* Production History

*Stay Safe!* was originally produced by The Lawrenceville School in partnership with the American High School Theatre Festival. It debuted at the 75th Edinburgh Festival Fringe in Edinburgh, Scotland for four performances in August, 2022.

The cast was as follows:

| | |
|---|---|
| ASTRID STARPEPPER | - Sofia Carlisi |
| WRENCH | - Eric Frankel |
| STEWARD | – Emily Hammond |
| TAILOR | – Claire Jiang |
| GYM | – Eddie Newsome |
| FLORA | – Anoushka Sharma |
| DEETS | – Naa Kwama Ankrah |
| BINS | - Sonia Lackey |
| TAB | – Sasha Mykhantso |
| MAN | – Jalen Lespinsasse |

The production was directed by Matthew R. Campbell. The Production Stage Manager was Autri Basu; Additional technical support was provided by Rania Shah, Sonia Singhal, and Cira Sar. The Company Manager was Karla Guido.

*STAY SAFE!*

*A burst of electric lights and exciting music—
like the opening of an anime car-racing video
game. In a flash of stars and glitter, ASTRID
STARPEPPER appears—magenta hair and
brightly colored dress and maybe a magic wand.
She greets the audience with her trademark
bubbly kawaii enthusiasm.*

ASTRID STARPEPPER:
Good good good evening everyone!
I'm Astrid Starpepper!

*A triumphant musical tag plays every time
ASTRID says her name.*

Wel Wel Welcome to the Denizen Isolation Security
Compound, or DISC!

In 2047, when the nuclear fallout rained down over the
nation, the surviving members of the government converted
this stay-stay-state-of-the-art scientific research facility into
a containment center for the most vulnerable in our society:
The children. Each DISC has been fit fit fitted to
accommodate eight irradiated patients—bio-irradiated, to be
exact. The radiation sickness infecting these patients has a
dormancy period that even scientists don't fully understand.
Some people develop symptoms right away, and for oth oth
other people, symptoms lay dormant for days, months, even
years! Thankfully, with the help a very special medicinal
regimen, the denizens of this facility have not exhibited any
symptoms at all! Whew! Let's give a cheer!

*An electronic crowd cheer, as if a digital car
crossed a virtual finish line in an imaginary
stadium.*

1

ASTRID STARPEPPER (cont):
Oh, poor bay-bay-babies, you're thinking, but no pity here!
Because in our DISC, each Denizen is taught a valuable skill
—a skill that has transferable properties out in the real
world. You'll see, our happy Denizens are raised to their
fullest potential—eagerly awaiting their reentry into society
once the threat of the radiation has been nul nul nullified!
And our top scientists are assuring us that we'll have a cure
to the radiation sickness in three to five day day day day day
decades! So sit tight, kids! You'll be back out on the
playground in no time!
I'm Astrid Starpepper—

*Musical tag.*

Stay safe, Everyone!

*She does a flourish. Maybe she vanishes with a
twinkle and a pop. The stage goes black,
accompanied by the sound of a television
monitor being shut off.*

*Silence.*

*One by one, lights buzz up on the Denizens:
DEETS scribbles in a notebook. It is one of
dozens. TAB assigns blue pills from a large
bottle into small cups with a pair of tweezers.
Eight cups, eight pills per cup. Each one clicks
as TAB drops it in. BINS is on the floor, asleep.
STEWARD stares into the VizCom out over the
audience, monitoring, monitoring. FLORA
hums, tracing a finger through the soil of a
window box of herbs.WRENCH and TAILOR are
pressed against the walls they have adjoining
GYM, who speaks, recounting a dream. TAILOR*

2

*is stitching a blanket; WRENCH is using a*
*screwdriver to repair Johnny Rockets.*

GYM:

I fall back, my arms outstretched, and the ground comes up
behind me, and it catches me like it was waiting for me. It's
bright green, the grass, and I am lying in it, facing up, and it
brushes the back of my neck like feathers, the hair at the
nape of my neck, and if I turn my head, it tickles my ears.

TAILOR:

It tickles?

GYM:

I guess.

WRENCH:

Keep going.

GYM:

The sky is blue and streaked with these long white clouds. It
stretches from one side of my eye to the other side of my
other eye, and it's so big, so wide, for a moment I lose
myself in the bigness of it all, like I'm a seashell and it's the
ocean—

*TAILOR:*
*(giddy)* I'm getting dizzy, Gym—stop it—

WRENCH:

Don't stop—keep going.

GYM:

And then, as I'm getting lost in the sky, I feel the grass beneath me start to move, the earth beneath me start to move, to roll, to rumble, but gentle, like I'm being rocked back and forth. I'm sinking in, like slowly sinking in, and the ground and the grass comes up my shoulders, and it tightens, ever so slowly, around my shoulders, around the sides of my head, around my legs, changing its shape to mold to the form of my body. Holding me. The ground has taken shape around me—

WRENCH:

Like a fitting?

TAILOR:

Like a thimble?

GYM:

Like arms, cradling me, like flesh, soft and cool, but not flesh because, duh, ground, and it's just green and brown and the sky is blue and white, and the golden beam of sun hits my face and I feel warmth on my nose and my cheeks and my forehead. And I close my eyes.

*Beat.*

And that's it.

TAILOR and WRENCH:

Wow.

*FLORA stops humming.*

TAILOR:

That's beautiful.

*They contemplate this. FLORA starts filling up*
*cups with water from a jug. BINS rolls over.*

GYM:

Tailor—it's your go.

TAILOR:

None of my dreams have color like your dreams have color.

GYM:

Sure they do.

TAILOR:

Is Wrench still listening?

GYM:

*(calling over)* Wrench?

WRENCH:

I'm here.

TAILOR:
Tell him that I'm sorry. Tell him that I know they'll come.

GYM:

Wrench?

WRENCH:
Is Tailor telling me she's sorry?

GYM:

She's sorry.

WRENCH:
Is she telling me she knows they'll come?

GYM:

Yeah.

WRENCH:

Again?

GYM:

Yup.

WRENCH:

You know what to say back.

GYM:

Wrench says he knows it too. He says thanks, Tailor.

WRENCH:

That's not it, Gym.

GYM:

Wrench says he thinks you're really nice, Tailor. He says he thinks he'll be dreaming before the end of the week.

TAILOR:

Aw, that's great!

GYM:

And he also said he thinks those dreams might be of you.

TAILOR:

What?

WRENCH:

Gym!

GYM:

He said he likes the way your eyes sparkle like the inhibitor lights on the compound doors.

WRENCH:

I did not!

TAILOR:

No he didn't.

GYM:

He said he bets you smell like fresh cut fruit and clouds on the wind and, I dunno, water from the ocean and—

WRENCH:

Shut up! Would you—

*DEETS interrupts.*

DEETS:

Excuse me—
Wrench? I'm trying to transcribe yesterday's recordings and you're just—
You're just distracting me.

WRENCH:

Sorry, Deets.
*(through the wall, to GYM)* We were too loud.

GYM:

My bad, Deets.

DEETS:

I can hear you through the wall, you're all—

WRENCH:

We'll quiet down, Deets. I promise.

GYM:

*(calling back)* What did you say?

WRENCH:

I told Deets we'd quiet down!

TAILOR:                                           DEETS:

What's happening right                You're the worst.

now?

> *Pause. DEETS goes back to writing. TAB begins*
> *snapping lids on each of the cups.*

WRENCH:

It's not worth it.

GYM:

What isn't?

WRENCH:

Dreaming. Grass and wind and clouds? Those things don't
exist to us anymore. We're never going to see them. We'll be
in here forever. Popping pills and muttering through walls.

GYM:

Someone's bitter.

WRENCH:

I'm not.

GYM:

Like, we're safe, we're healthy, we have food and water and
everything.

WRENCH:

I know.

GYM:

You make it sound like we're in a prison or something.

WRENCH:

Sometimes it feels that way. Wake up at this time. Eat at this time. Take pills at this time.

GYM:

Do you know what would happen if you stopped taking your meds?

WRENCH:

No.

GYM:

Neither do I. But I bet you money it would suck.

WRENCH:

Neither of us have money.

GYM:

I bet you a sock.

> *STEWARD speaks into the VizCom. A chime sounds in each room. The Denizens all turn out to the audience, except for BINS, who remains asleep.*

STEWARD:

Three minutes to Dark, everyone. Tab?

TAB:

Just finishing up.

STEWARD:

Wrench—how is Johnny Rockets?

WRENCH:

The wiring between the power module and the receiver had loosened up. Nothing too traumatic. He's ready to make delivery runs again.

STEWARD:

You figured it out pretty quickly.

WRENCH:

You can solve any problem once you realize machines are all cause and effect.

STEWARD:

And humans are the most complicated machines of them all. Tab, you ready to solve our problems?

TAB:

Ready.

STEWARD:

Flora?

FLORA:

Water's ready.

STEWARD:

Okay then. Send Johnny.

*WRENCH presses a few buttons on the VizCom panel, and JOHNNY ROCKETS emerges. JOHNNY orbits the rooms until it reaches FLORA. Carefully, FLORA gives JOHNNY the cups of water, keeping one for herself. JOHNNY distributes them outside each delivery port. Then JOHNNY orbits to TAB, and retrieves the medication. JOHNNY distributes the meds to each port. JOHNNY powers down.*

STEWARD (cont):
Pills and water in your delivery ports.

DEETS:

Bins.

STEWARD:

What?

DEETS:

Bins is asleep.

STEWARD:
Bins? Bins! Rise and shine so we can go to bed. Flora—give the wall a knock or two?

*FLORA pounds on the wall with a trowel.*

FLORA:

Bins! Get up!

*BINS stirs.*

BINS:

What?

FLORA:

Night meds.

BINS:

Day meds?

FLORA:
Night meds. We've only got two minutes left.

DEETS:

One minute, thirty-seven.

BINS:

Whatever.

STEWARD:

Quick now. Everybody. One at a time. Down the hatch.
Eight.
Seven.
Six.

*WRENCH drops one. It rolls away.*

Five.
Four.

WRENCH:

I dropped one.

*They wait.*

Got it.

STEWARD:

Good.

WRENCH

Sorry.

STEWARD:

Three.
Two.
One.

*The Denizens have swallowed each pill. All
except WRENCH, who still holds several of them
in his hand.*

STEWARD (cont):
Take your meds, Wrench.

*WRENCH stares at them.*

Take them, Wrench.

TAB:                              TAILOR:
Take your medicine, please.      Holy cow, Wrench—

DEETS:                           GYM:
Wrench—                          Dude, come on!

*Wrench brings his hand to his face, consuming
all the pills at once. He chases them with the
water. Makes a show of it.*

STEWARD:

All gone?

WRENCH:

All gone, Stew.

STEWARD:
What is your problem, Wrench?

WRENCH:
I don't have a problem.

STEWARD:
We don't want anyone to get sick. No one gets sick.

*WRENCH thinks.*

STEWARD (cont):
No one gets sick. Got it?

WRENCH:
No one gets sick.

STEWARD:
Good.

GYM:
Serious, Wrench. Don't even joke like that.

TAB:
What were you thinking?

WRENCH:
I wasn't.
It was just... a momentary lapse.

TAB:
Your momentary lapse could result in you getting fevers.
Nausea. Increased chance of infection. Internal bleeding.
Organ failure.

WRENCH:
Okay, Tab—

TAB:
It's not okay. Bioradiation Poisoning isn't a joke. It's a killer.
We're not immune just because we're in here.

GYM:
Relax, Tab.

WRENCH:
Sorry, Tab.

TAB:

If you collapse, no one is here to help you. No one can get to you to help you.

STEWARD:

Take a breath, Tab.

*TAB takes a breath.*

TAB:

Moron. Utter moron.

STEWARD:

All right everyone, it's time to power down. Stay safe and Healthy, everyone.

> *A chorus of "Stay safe and Healthy," as one by one, TAILOR, DEETS, FLORA, GYM, and TAB turns off their lights.*

We're going dark in ten seconds whether you like it or not, Wrench.

> *WRENCH says nothing.*

> *The lights go out. In the darkness, a dim light comes up on WRENCH, stock still, staring into his open palm. And in it, several little blue pills. He puts them on the floor. WRENCH pulls Johnny Rockets into the cell. He grabs the screwdriver and tightens screws all over the little robot.*

WRENCH:

You did good today, buddy.

"Thank you, Wrench."

You know, when you malfunction, I can take you apart. Strip you down, remove your plating and investigate every fuse, every connection, every actuator. I look to the most basic elements of your construction to find the issue, so I can fix you and get you functional again.

What if... what if my inability to dream is a malfunction? What if it's the result of something within me that's broken? Steward said: Humans are the most complicated machines of them all.

That's what she said.

If I'm going to find out why I don't dream, I'll need to get back to the most basic version of me. I need to get to the Wrench that existed before the DISC, before the virus, before the... pills. I need to get to the most basic version of who I am.

Maybe then I can see at least some version of the world I imagine.

> *WRENCH snaps open a compartment on Johnny, places the pills within, and closes it.*

It's just for one day.

I'm sure I'll be fine.

"You'll be fine, Wrench."

Thanks, Johnny.

> *WRENCH returns Johnny back outside the delivery port, closes it.*
>
> *Black.*
>
> *For a moment, nothing, then a dim light comes up on BINS, standing in the darkness, stretching her muscles. At last, in the silence, BINS reaches*

*to the floor, and pulls up a metal panel with
rusty creak. BINS vanishes into the hole.*

*Lights go dark again. Then Johnny Rockets' eyes
begin to glow.*

*The sound of radio static. Of waves of static,
getting louder and softer, louder and softer, and
then, cutting through the static, a MAN's voice.*

### MAN:

Can anyone hear me?
Can anyone hear me?
If you can hear me, please say something. Just one thing.
Don't you want to be free?
Don't you want to see the world again?
If you do, follow the sound. Follow the sound of my voice.
Reach out—
Reach out your hand—
Please, Elias.
Please.

*A pause.*

Nothing.
I don't know what I expected—I don't know what—

*The MAN sighs.*

As long as it takes.

*Static, moving in and out—and then gone.
Johnny's eyes go dark. Silence.*

*The dim light flicks on, and WRENCH sits
upright in the room, eyes wide with shock.*

*Blackout.*

*Lights and music burst up with a flourish on
ASTRID STARPEPPER, in the center of the
DISC. Her hair is purple; her dress is a different
color too.*

ASTRID STARPEPPER:
Goo goo good morning, Denizens! It's me, Astrid
Starpepper!

*Musical flourish.*

It's the fourteenth day of July; six-thirty in the morning, and
it's time to start the day! Let's go go go!

*Pumping House music starts as the lights come
up on the Denizens. They are groggy, still half
asleep.*

Take it away, Gym!

*GYM pops up and springs into action.*

GYM:
Okay, everyone! Let's get our blood flowing!

*Everyone but BINS gets up to do the workout—
BINS half-asses the motions from bed. GYM
leads them through a series of calisthenics and
aerobic exercises in time with the music.
ASTRID does it with them. Throughout, GYM
gives them encouraging aerobics instructor
advice.*

*At last, mercifully, the music stops.*

GYM (cont):
That's it! Walk it out, everybody.

*The Denizens mostly do a cooldown, some stretch.*

*ASTRID shows no sign of fatigue, of course.*

ASTRID STARPEPPER:
Great jah jah job everyone! Now it's time for sup sup supplements and hydration! Vocational instruction will begin in three three three three two hours! See you then! This is Astrid Starpepper—

*Musical flourish.*

Saying: Stay safe, everyone!

*ASTRID blips and vanishes, leaving the Denizens alone.*

STEWARD:
You heard the lady. Time for drugs.

TAB:
On it.

*TAB begins laying out cups; as does FLORA.*

WRENCH:
Hey guys--?

STEWARD:
Deets—what day is it?

DEETS:
July the—

WRENCH:
Guys—you'll never believe—

STEWARD:
No, like what day of the week—

DEETS:
Wrench, it's hard for me to hear—

WRENCH:
Sorry!

DEETS:
It's a Sunday.

STEWARD:
Sunday. Right! We have individual virtual instruction in two hours, with a twenty-minute reduction for Sunday recreation. Flora, let's get breakfast out and about. What's on the menu?

FLORA:
Salad. It's always salad.

*A half-hearted YAY from mostly everyone.*

TAB:
Salad is, like, the math of food.

GYM:
I'm gonna pretend my salad has meat in it.

WRENCH:
Steward—

STEWARD:
Wrench—send Johnny to Flora?

WRENCH:

Yeah, okay.

STEWARD:

Now then, Wrench—you wanted to say--?

WRENCH:

I had a dream last night.

*They all stop. Even BINS sits up.*

I was here, I was here in bed, and then I heard a voice. A man's voice. And he was asking me all these questions. He was telling me to reach out, telling me to reach towards something, and I remember thinking, reach towards what?

*FLORA looks down, suddenly uncomfortable. DEETS' pen freezes.*

And then he said something about not giving up—and he sounded so sad. "As long as it takes," he said. And then I woke up.

*Beat.*

GYM:

Well that sounds...

TAB:

Thrilling.

*TAB continues to put pills in cups.*

WRENCH:

Okay, okay—it's not, like, so exciting. But it's my first dream since I can remember. My first since...

*WRENCH trails off.*

It was actually pretty scary.
Are any of your dreams scary?

TAILOR:
Sometimes mine are.

BINS:
Not me. Mine are like flying in a sea of beans.

WRENCH:
Oh.

STEWARD:
It sounds like a good dream, Wrench.

TAB:
Yeah. Well done on that thing you have no control over.

GYM:
It's a starter dream. You're just out of practice.

WRENCH:
It's been so long since I...
I thought I was broken.

*They shift uncomfortably.*

BINS:
I'm going back to sleep.

STEWARD:
Okay, everyone—Shall we?

*Blackout.*

*Lights come up on FLORA's room, fully
illuminated. She is tending her window box of
herbs, but it's clear she is distracted. She stops,
speaks into the VizCom.*

FLORA:
Open private communication to Deets.

*A chime, and lights up on DEETS, who is
writing furiously.*

Deets--?

DEETS:
I'm writing.

FLORA:
Deets, did you hear what he said? What Wrench said?

DEETS:
Did you hear what I said? I'm writing.

FLORA:
What could possibly be so important—?

DEETS:
Astrid is having me write a history of the 2045 Insurrection
—on top of chronicling everything that is going on inside
our DISC. I've had to watch numerous documentaries on the
primary agitators and their agendas, including their efforts to
overthrow the presidency and the subsequent nuclear
incident, and now I've been instructed to condense and
simplify those pages so all of you can learn about it.

FLORA:

Why would we need to learn about some weird historical thing that happened when we were, like, two?

DEETS:

I don't know. Ask the Virtual Superguide system why my Vocational Instruction requires me to do homework until my fingers ache, and yours requires you to sit next to a pile of dirt until lettuce happens.

FLORA:

Happens?

DEETS:

Sprouts. Whatever.

FLORA:

Look, Deets—I need you to talk to me.

DEETS:

There's nothing to discuss.

FLORA:

Stop writing and look up. Look up at me. Please.

> *Slowly, DEETS puts down the pen and looks up at FLORA on the VizCom.*

What do we do?

DEETS:

We do nothing.

FLORA:

It happened to Wrench.

DEETS:

It's purely coincidental.

FLORA:

That's not a coincidence.

DEETS:

No. It's a dream. You heard what Wrench said--

FLORA:

You've written down everything we've said or done since—

DEETS:

Eleven years.

FLORA:

Eleven years!
And in that time, how many dreams have you logged?

DEETS:

Three thousand seventy-two.

FLORA:

And how many of those were like this?

*DEETS blanches. She doesn't know what to say.*

I told you it wasn't my fault.

DEETS:

It doesn't matter--

FLORA:

It wasn't your fault, it wasn't my fault, it—

DEETS:
We promised we wouldn't talk about it, Flora. I don't want to be punished. Not again.

FLORA:
I have to know.

DEETS:
I don't!

FLORA:
Of course you do. I'm the one who's supposed to grow stuff; you're the one who's supposed to know stuff.

*She speaks into the VizCom*

Open private communication to Wrench.

*A chime, and lights up on Wrench, deep in thought as he polishes Johnny Rockets with a rag.*

WRENCH:
Hey, Flora. Hi Deets.

DEETS:
Hello.

WRENCH:
Can I ask you guys a question?

FLORA:
Sure.

WRENCH:

I'm worried. About my dream?
I only ask because I'm trying to make sure I didn't mess
something up, you know?

DEETS:

Tailor said her dreams were sometimes scary.

WRENCH:

But that's Tailor. She might have said that to be nice, you
know?

DEETS:

I guess.

WRENCH:

Tab thought it was boring. You could hear it in his voice.

FLORA:

Maybe.

WRENCH:

But it wasn't. Not to me.
I'm just trying to figure it all out.

FLORA:

Well, how about we talk about it?
About your dream. Together.

WRENCH:

You think that'll help?

*WRENCH looks at DEETS through the VizCom.*

Deets?
Why aren't you writing anything down?

FLORA:
Last night. In the dream. You said you heard a voice?

WRENCH:
Yeah—it was tinny, like, a little far away? A man's voice.

FLORA:
And he was asking you questions?

WRENCH:
Yeah.

FLORA:
Do you remember what he asked you?

WRENCH:
Vaguely.

FLORA:
"Don't you want to be free?"
"Don't you want to see the world again?"

*Beat.*

WRENCH:
How...
How could you know that?

FLORA:
Wrench. Did you take your meds last night?

*Wrench is caught off guard.*

DEETS:
Don't answer that.

FLORA:

Sorry!

DEETS:

Flora, you know better than to—

WRENCH:

I don't think it's a big deal—

DEETS:

Wrench, shut up.

WRENCH:

If it makes it any better, I don't feel—

DEETS:

Wrench!!
Stop speaking.

*WRENCH stops speaking.*

If you answer, she'll hear.

FLORA:

There are words, combinations of words, phrases that trigger her.

WRENCH:

Who?

DEETS:

She can hear everything that gets said or transmitted through the VizCom. But there are a few things that are transmitted directly to her.

FLORA:

It's not safe.

WRENCH:
So what? So what if she hears? What can she possibly—

*With a burst of music and glitter and light,*
*ASTRID STARPEPPER appears. Lights come up*
*on the rest of the Denizens as well.*

ASTRID STARPEPPER:
Good afternoon, my happy Denizens!

TAB:
What's going on?

TAILOR:
Is it time already?

STEWARD:
It's a surprise—

ASTRID STARPEPPER:
Sur sur surprise instruction! Today we're going to hear all
about the deadly nuke nuke nuclear detonation that
decimated the population! Again! If you'll all apply your
Hearpiece, we'll begin.

*Each of the Denizens inserts earbuds into their*
*ears, and sits up facing their respective VizCom*
*screens. DEETS and FLORA are particularly*
*anxious.*

*An audio recording begins, with a musical*
*flourish, and the voice of ASTRID. This*
*documentary-style monologue continues quietly*
*underneath the entire following scene.*

ASTRID (VO):
In the year 2045, a faction of anti-nationalist left-wing propagandists began a systematic assault on the freedoms and liberties of the American people. Utilizing Communistic brainwashing techniques to push back against the policies of the government, the insurrectionists pursued an aggressive agenda of activism, re-education, and mandatory empathy. Their platform included weakening the borders, reducing religious liberties, and eliminating police and security forces.

Naturally, the federal government responded definitively, commandeering left-wing propagandist news organizations, arresting publishers, artists, college professors and proponents of these protests, and disbanding community centers and churches designed to harbor such criminals.

But the insurrectionists would not be deterred. On March 14th, 2047, left-wing radicals unleashed a coordinated bio-nuclear attack in cities across the nation. The radiation killed thousands and poisoned tens of thousands more. For many, the effects lay dormant in its victims for days, months, even years. But once symptoms begin to appear, victims might have only hours to live.

The response was quick, resulting in curfews, segregation, and thousands of detentions, but it was too late to stop the waves of illness rampaging the nation. Medical facilities capable of containing the bioradiation sickness were constructed to provide a haven to the most vulnerable in our population: the children.

> *The lights fade on all but WRENCH. ASTRID steps into WRENCH's cell. Her demeanor has changed—from sunny anime princess to menacing predator. As the above VO plays:*

ASTRID:

Hell hell hell hello, Wrench.

WRENCH:

Um... hello?

ASTRID:

It has come to our attention that you neglected to take your medications last night.

WRENCH:

I didn't mean to—

ASTRID:

Surely you understand that by not taking your med med medications you're putting yourself at risk of serious illness.

WRENCH:

I feel fine.

ASTRID:

The radiation is still inside you, Wrench. It is still a part of you. We can never know when it will begin to attack your body. But we know for sure that it will. At some point, it will.

WRENCH:

I get it.

ASTRID:

Do do do you? Because if you fail to take your medicine, the bio-radiation sickness will kill you. Your death will be painful. Dizziness. Vomiting. There is blood. So much blood.

WRENCH:

I get it.

ASTRID:

Without you, Wrench, Johnny Rockets will fail to function. Your friends will no longer be able to receive food. Water. Or their own medicine. Your foolish decision will lead to all all all of their deaths. Do you understand?

WRENCH:

I... I guess so.

ASTRID:

Such behavior cannot be tolerated. Punishment is unavoidable.

WRENCH:

Punishment?

ASTRID:

Maybe next time you'll show some consideration for your peers, Wrench.
Maybe next time you'll think.

> *The lights in WRENCH's cell goes out. The sound of an electric jolt, and WRENCH cries out in pain.*

> *The stage is black as the documentary voice of ASTRID concludes.*

ASTRID (VO):

Scientists say a cure to the dormant radiation sickness may be developed within the next several years, so we can all hope that their lonely quarantines will be over soon, and we can welcome them back into our society with open arms. But until then, Stay Safe, Everyone!

> *A flourish of music and the stage is left silent, in black.*

*That evening. Lights come on everyone but*
*WRENCH. DEETS is scribbling in a notebook.*
*FLORA is filling cups with water from her tank.*
*TAB is doling out pills into cups. Eight cups,*
*eight pills per cup; GYM is doing crunches.*
*BINS is asleep. TAILOR speaks into the VizCom*
*to STEWARD. She has a bowl of salad that she*
*has been pushing around with a fork.*


### TAILOR:
I'm worried.

### STEWARD:
I know.

### TAILOR:
Can you try again?

### STEWARD:
Every time I try to reach him, I get—

*The disembodied voice of ASTRID*
*STARPEPPER.*

### ASTRID STARPEPPER (VO):
The VizCom of... Wrench... is temporarily offline due to
maintenance. Please be patient.

### STEWARD:
See?

### TAILOR:
It's been hours.

STEWARD:

I'm sure everything's fine. He'll be back online by the morning.

*(noticing)* Tailor—you didn't eat anything?

*She looks down at her bowl.*

TAILOR:

I haven't been very hungry.

STEWARD:

Maybe you're getting sick of salads. I sure am.

*From next door, FLORA perks up.*

FLORA:

It's not like I can grow steak in here.

STEWARD:

Point taken, Flora.

FLORA:

Hey—if you're on with Tailor, tell her I gave her an extra tomato at the bottom of her bowl. Tell her I knew she'd be worried about Wrench, so I gave her a little extra.

TAILOR:

I can hear her. Tell her I said thank you.

STEWARD:

She says thank you.

FLORA:

Remind her, Steward. Check the bottom of the bowl.

STEWARD:

She heard you.
Is the water all set?

FLORA:

Almost.

> *STEWARD presses a button to communicate*
> *with all the denizens.*

STEWARD

Everyone—it's about seven minutes to Dark. Tab, you got
everything under control?

TAB:

Nothing changes, Steward: Salad, pills, sleep; Salad, pills,
sleep.

STEWARD:

Just say yes or no.

> *TAB grumbles.*

*(to the group)* Since Wrench is unavailable, I'll activate
Johnny in five minutes. We good?

> *A chorus of Yeahs, Sures, etc. TAILOR leans*
> *towards the wall she shares with GYM. She*
> *pushes around the salad in her bowl.*

TAILOR:

Gym?

GYM:

What?

TAILOR:
Have you heard from Wrench?

GYM:
Not since our surprise instruction.

TAILOR:
Can you check, please?

GYM:
Check what?

TAILOR:
To see if he's okay.

GYM:
He's fine, Tailor.

TAILOR:
No one has been able to reach him since this morning—

GYM:
Don't you have a blanket to stitch or something?

TAILOR:
Just knock on the wall. Please?

GYM:
And say what?

TAILOR:
Tell him—
Tell him not to be embarrassed. About the dream.
Tell him that sometimes I have scary dreams, too.
Tell him that once, I had a dream where we were all trapped
in a metal shipping container, we were on our way
somewhere, and we were together, and we were trapped in a

TAILOR (cont):
shipping container with... with ourselves. Like there was
more than one of us? We were there, but if you looked to one
side, we were also there? And then the top of the container
was, like, ripped off, peeled off like a can opening, and a
bright light blinded us from above, and each of us were
pulled out into the air, away from ourselves, away from our
other selves, and we were dragged out, screaming, reaching
for our hands, reaching—
I remember so much screaming, so much...

GYM:
C'mon, Tailor. You want me to say all that?

> *TAILOR pulls away from the wall. She glumly
> pushes the salad around in the bowl.*

Tailor?
Tailor...

> *TAB snaps the lid on the final cup.
> Something at the bottom of the bowl catches
> TAILOR's eye.*

TAB:
Steward. I'm all set.

STEWARD:
Activating Johnny.

TAILOR:
What... what is this?

> *TAILOR finds a piece of paper at the bottom of
> the bowl. JOHNNY orbits the rooms until it
> reaches FLORA. Carefully, FLORA gives*

> *JOHNNY the cups of water, keeping one for*
> *herself.*

"Don't take your meds."

> *JOHNNY distributes them at the end of each*
> *room. Then JOHNNY orbits to TAB, and*
> *retrieves the medication.*

"Don't take...?"

> *JOHNNY distributes the meds to each room, and*
> *powers down outside TAILOR's cell.*

### STEWARD:

Everybody ready?

> *TAILOR tries to speak to FLORA through the*
> *VizCom.*

### TAILOR:

Flora?

### STEWARD:

Three minutes to Dark, guys.

### TAILOR:

Flora—what is this?

### DEETS:

Two minutes, forty-three seconds.

### FLORA:

I gave you an extra tomato.

### STEWARD:

Can somebody wake up Bins?

TAILOR:
Flora—what are you asking--?

BINS:
I'm up. I'm up.

STEWARD:
Then let's do this.
Eight.
Seven.

TAILOR:
Flora—

STEWARD:
Six.
Five.

FLORA:
Trust me.

STEWARD:
Less chatting, more pill swallowing, please.

TAILOR and FLORA:
Sorry.

STEWARD:
Four.
Three.
Two.
One.

*Neither FLORA nor TAILOR swallow any of the
pills. FLORA has dropped them into her water*

*cup. TAILOR has dropped them into her uneaten salad.*

STEWARD (cont):
Are we all good?
It's been a day. Tomorrow is Monday, so you know what that means: Dropdowns from the Outside. New thread and fabrics for Tailor, new seeds and soil for Flora, new journals for Deets, new tools and parts for...
Well, I'm sure Wrench will be back online soon and he'll get everything he needs. Tab—you remembered—

TAB:
Of course I remembered.

STEWARD:
Then there's nothing left but to say good night.
Stay Safe and Healthy, everyone!

*DEETS, GYM, FLORA, and TAB respond with "Stay Safe," or "Stay Safe and Healthy," as they click off their lights. BINS says nothing, but clicks off the light as well.*

TAILOR:
*(to herself)* What am I doing?

STEWARD:
Good night, Tailor.

TAILOR:
Good... good night.

STEWARD:
Wrench will be fine, Tailor. You'll see.

TAILOR:

Thank you, Steward.

> *STEWARD turns off the light. TAILOR reaches down and takes a pill from the salad bowl. She stares at it. She stares at it. Blackout.*
>
> *A dim light comes up in BINS' room. BINS opens a panel in the floor with a creak, disappears down into the hole. Blackout.*
>
> *A dim light comes up in FLORA's room. She pours the water into her window box of herbs. Blackout.*
>
> *A dim light comes up in TAILOR's room. She has lined the pills up in a row. She stares at them in the darkness.*
>
> *Once again, cutting through the darkness, radio static. And then again, a MAN's voice, slightly more resigned than before. Outside the cell, Johnny's eyes begin to glow.*

MAN:

Can anyone hear me?
Can anyone hear me?

> *TAILOR sits up straight.*

Please. If anyone is there—

TAILOR:

I'm here.

> *Silence.*

MAN:

You're here?

TAILOR:

Yes.

MAN:

Oh my God—
I can't believe—

TAILOR:

Please—not so loud—

MAN:

I'm so sorry, I've just been trying for so long—

TAILOR:

Quiet!
Please.

*Beat.*

MAN:

Are you—are you still there?

TAILOR:

I'm here.

MAN:

I thought… I thought it was my imagination.

TAILOR:

How are you doing this?

MAN:

Doing what?

TAILOR:

Talking... to me.

MAN:

There's a radio transmitter and receiver inside Johnny
Rockets.

Johnny Rockets eyes begin to glow with a pale
yellow light.

It's too small for the security system to detect, and since it's
communication through radio waves, it's virtually invisible
to the DISC security systems. It's old technology.

TAILOR:

From before.

MAN:

Yes.
Can I ask... what is your name?

TAILOR:

It's Tailor.

MAN:

Tailor.
I'm sorry if we've frightened you, Tailor.
My name is Kent.

TAILOR:

Um, hi.

KENT:

We've been waiting to hear from you nearly every day for—
for years.

TAILOR:

We?

KENT:

We want to help you get out of the DISC. My colleagues and
I.

TAILOR:

Colleagues?

KENT:

Yes.

TAILOR:

What does that mean?

KENT:

Ah—we are concerned citizens. We're a group of…
conscientious objectors.

TAILOR:

*(beneath her breath)* Insurrectionists.

KENT:

What? No—nothing like that. I was one of the architects of
the DISC.

*Beat.*

Tailor?

TAILOR:

You're trying to hurt us.

KENT:

Why would I want to hurt you? I want to save you?

TAILOR:
You want us to leave the DISC. But we know it's not safe.

KENT:
We'll do our best to protect you. But we need you and the others to—

TAILOR:
From the radiation sickness? We don't have gas masks or protective clothing. All we have are medications. How can you protect us?

KENT:
Tailor—
What radiation?

*Beat.*

What radiation sickness are you talking about?
There's no radiation out here.
Are you sick?

TAILOR:
There's... no radiation?

KENT:
I mean, they threatened us with all sorts of punishments, but I don't think even they could get away with—

TAILOR:
Threatened you?

*Beat.*

KENT:
Tailor, what do you remember about your life before the DISC?

TAILOR:

I don't... I don't understand.

KENT:

Do you remember your parents?

TAILOR:

There's no radiation?

KENT:

Tailor—

TAILOR:

How can that be true?

KENT:

Please, listen to me. I need you to convince the others. I need you to convince the others to reach out. To reach out their hands towards the sound of my voice—

TAILOR:

I don't understand anything you're saying.

> *Suddenly, a metal clang, like a grate slamming shut. TAILOR jumps.*

KENT:

What was that?

TAILOR:

I have to go.

KENT:

Tailor, please—

TAILOR:
I have to go. You have to go.


KENT:
Please! We are trying to help you!


TAILOR:
No—I don't know who you are or what you want. You're
criminals. You're using a brainwashing technique on me.
This was a mistake.

> *TAILOR grabs all the pills from the floor and
> swallows them.*


KENT:
Tailor? Tailor—talk to us. Talk to us! Tailor!
Is there a boy—?
Is there a boy named Elias with you?
Please!

> *As TAILOR passes out, static starts to edge its
> way in, and then the MAN's voice is lost. Static.
> Johnny's eyes go dark.*

> *The same night, but later. A portable lantern
> reveals WRENCH's cell. WRENCH is up against
> the wall, knees to his chest, still in considerable
> physical pain. BINS stands over him, unsure as
> to why WRENCH is awake. They stare at each
> other in the darkness. BINS wears a mask and
> rubber gloves, holds a spray bottle and a cloth.*


BINS:
Uh.
Hey.

WRENCH:

Bins?
What are you doing here?

BINS:

I could be asking you the same thing.
Normally when I come up, you're passed out like everyone else.

WRENCH:

Normally?

BINS:

Sundays, Tuesdays, Fridays.

*They stare at each other for a moment.*

This is awkward.
I'm just going to clean your room, if that's cool.

WRENCH:

Uh, sure.

BINS:

Don't worry about the mask. It's more to protect me than to protect you.

WRENCH:

I see.

*BINS begins cleaning the room. Spraying with the spray bottle, wiping down with the cloth.*

BINS:

I noticed your meds were still outside your room's delivery port. I got them for you.

*BINS hands WRENCH the cup of pills.*

WRENCH:
Thanks.

BINS:
*(a realization)* That's why you're still up! I get it. I don't know what most of these pills do, but there's definitely one that knocks you on your ass.

WRENCH:
Don't you take them?

BINS:
I take the morning ones at night and the night ones in the morning, as per my instruction from Her Majesty, the Great and Powerful Hologramus Virtual Astrid Starpepper.

*BINS scrubs.*

I probably wasn't supposed to tell you that.

WRENCH:
Bins—have you ever wondered if the pills actually do anything? If they actually keep us safe?

BINS:
I never really thought about it. But none of us have ever gotten sick, so I guess it works.

WRENCH:
I guess.

BINS:

I mean, if the medication doesn't do anything, like, then what's the point? Why keep us here? This entire set up has got to be crazy expensive, right? The pills are supposed to keep the radiation sickness in check so we don't get sick, and we live in the DISC so to keep us from encountering other people who might expose us. Right? That makes sense to me. We take these drugs to protect ourselves and others. Which is cool. But if the pills don't do anything, then we're not here because we're a danger to society. Then we've been isolated from each other... for what? We're here because... I don't know. I don't even know.

WRENCH:

I don't know either.

BINS:

And if that's the case, then I've been cleaning and sterilizing and wiping down all your rooms every night for as long as I can remember, avoiding contact with everyone, singing myself to sleep every night, for what? For nothing? If I've been doing all this work for nothing, that would reaaaaaaallly piss me off. I mean, wouldn't it piss you off?

WRENCH:

How do you get into our rooms?

BINS:

There are grates in the floor that lift up—if you have the key *(she jingles it from a chain around her neck)*—and a tunnel underneath the whole DISC. Where I hang out.

WRENCH:

You hang out?

BINS:

Of course! I mean, I'm not all, like, scrubbing and mopping.
I'm not just my vocation. I... uh... I like to draw? And I have
this, um, disinfectant that dries, like, white? So sometimes,
I'll use it like ink, and draw on the walls? Like, sometimes I
draw you guys or I'll try to draw Astrid—which is pretty
hard because she's always moving, and you guys are usually
asleep—
This probably sounds pretty stupid.

WRENCH:

It doesn't. It doesn't at all.

BINS:

No?
Cool.
Thanks, Wrench.
You're a pretty nice person.
It's actually really nice talking to someone. Like, face to
face. Mask to face.

WRENCH:

It is.
Hey, Bins, have you ever heard voices? At night? Like, a
man's voice? Asking if we want to be free?

BINS:

Oh, sure. Last night. Tonight, too. And then pretty much
three or four times a week for, like, years and years.

WRENCH:

It wasn't a dream.

BINS:

It stopped for a while and then it came back. But I don't know how to answer, so I never said anything. I always figured it was something we could get in trouble for, so I steered clear.

WRENCH:

I was hoping...
I was hoping it was a dream.

BINS:

Why?

WRENCH:

I haven't had a dream since before we came to the DISC, I think.

BINS:

Was there a before? I don't even remember.

WRENCH:

It might have been a memory.

BINS:

Aren't they the same thing? They're both invented by your brain to process something. When it's a memory, it's something from the past, and when it's a dream, it's something about the present, but it's basically the same thing.
I like to draw animals. I imagine what they would feel like if I touched their fur or their feathers. I remember informational sessions that Astrid showed us about animals and then I dream about petting a dog or combing the hair on a horse and I'm like, is this a dream, or a did I, like, actually do this before? Or did I just invent it out of nowhere? And by then I'm usually pretty hungry, so I'll go to Flora's room and steal a tomato.

*Beat.*

#### WRENCH:

I just want...
I just want to see the sky.
I just want to see the trees.
I want...
Even in a dream.
Even if it's only in a dream.

#### BINS:

I get it.
I really do.
But then again, I spend every night sniffing cleaning solution
and my best friend is a drawing of a puppy named Clorox.
So maybe don't listen to me.

*Silence.*

*BINS reaches out her gloved hands and, after a
moment, WRENCH takes them in his own. They
remain like that for a moment. BINS standing,
WRENCH sitting, just holding the other's hands.
At last, BINS pulls back.*

Thank you, Bins.

#### BINS:

No problem, Wrench.

*BINS takes the spray bottle, sprays her gloved
hands. She wipes them on the cloth.*

I'm gonna need you to move so I can get to that part of the
floor.

*Blackout.*

*Music and lights burst up around ASTRID STARPEPPER, glowing and radiant in electric blue hair. Is that a different dress, too? Where does she get them all?*

ASTRID STARPEPPER:
Precautions and protections, am I ri ri right? That's where it's at! We cannot be a civil society with a nuke nuke nuclear incident happening every other minute! Exposure to toxic levels of bioradiation results in deaths too gruesome to imagine. It can lay dormant inside the human body for for for forever, maybe: We just don't know! That's why your government has put these mandates in place for all Denizens across the nation: Stay inside, filter your air, wash your food, wash your house, wash your mail, work from home, boil your water, and most importantly, NO TUH TUH TOUCHING. If you follow these strict guidelines and take your double daily dose of medicay-cay-cations, you will find yourself radiation-free!

*Thunderous applause.*

Stay Safe Ev Ev Every--!

*ASTRID blips out as she is interrupted by STEWARD, who speaks through the VizCom to WRENCH. The others—all except TAILOR—listen in. TAILOR can't bear to look at the screen.*

STEWARD:
So it wasn't a dream.

WRENCH:
No.

STEWARD:

You're sure?

FLORA:

I heard them too, Steward.

WRENCH:

And Bins.

BINS:

I'm supposed to be, like, asleep right now?

STEWARD:

"Don't you want to be free?"
"Don't you want to see the world again?"

WRENCH:

That's what they asked.

FLORA:

Tailor heard him, too.
I couldn't make out what he was saying, but I could hear her
talking to him. Last night.

STEWARD:

Tailor?
Tailor, is that true?

TAILOR:

I don't know what's true.

STEWARD:

But did you hear voices? A man's voice?

TAILOR:

Maybe.

                              TAB:
Maybe? Or yes?

                             TAILOR:
Yes, Tab.

                            STEWARD:
And you spoke to them?

                             TAILOR:
Yes.

                            STEWARD:
What did they say to you?

                             TAILOR:
I don't want to talk about it.

                              GYM:
Tailor?

                             TAILOR:
I don't want to talk about it.

                              TAB:
I find this all very suspicious.

                             WRENCH:
Which part?

                              TAB:
The whole thing! A strange man has been attempting to
contact us with the express intent of "freeing" us? That's not
sounding any alarms for you?

STEWARD:

It does for me.


WRENCH:

Bins has been hearing them on and off for years.


BINS:

I tend to ignore weird stuff.


TAB:

Why didn't you say anything, Flora?
Seriously? Why didn't you or Deets say anything then?


FLORA:

Do you wake up and announce to everyone every thought
you've ever had in the middle of the night?


GYM:

I do.


TAB:

I'm sorry, is this a joke? Are you all making this up?


WRENCH:

It's not a joke.


GYM:

It does sound crazy.


TAB:

Where does the voice even come from?


TAILOR:

There's a radio transmitter and receiver inside Johnny
Rockets.

## WRENCH:

*(geeking out)* Of course! I must have activated it when I was doing the repairs. I thought it was in case the satellite signals burnt out we'd still be able to get information from Astrid— but this makes so much more sense!

## STEWARD:

To you, maybe.

Look, I'm not saying this didn't happen, but I would be an idiot if I weren't skeptical. I think we should report it.

## FLORA and WRENCH:

No!

## STEWARD:

Like it or not, we don't know if these voices are trustworthy. We don't know if they are messing with us or have other sinister intentions.

## FLORA:

"Sinister intentions?"

## TAB:

They could be insurrectionists.

## STEWARD:

The Communists who set off the nuclear devices.

## GYM:

You think they're still out there?

## WRENCH:

If you report it, Tailor will be punished.

## TAB:

Punished?

WRENCH:

We'll all be punished.

DEETS:

Wrench—stop.

WRENCH:

To the tune of 250 volts.

GYM:

Wait, what?

FLORA:

We don't know that that's going to happen—

GYM:

250 volts?

STEWARD:

Stop it.

WRENCH:

Do you wanna know what that feels like?

BINS:

Hard pass.

TAB:

Maybe you deserved it.

FLORA:

What did you just say?

DEETS:

Flora—

STEWARD:
Stop it! All of you. Stop it.
We don't know anything. We don't know anything about what life is like outside the DISC, other than the fact that the atmosphere is still toxic out there, and here, even if we're uncomfortable, at least we are safe. Our safety is the most important thing.

WRENCH:
If there are people out there, then there must be a way for them to protect themselves.

STEWARD:
We don't know that.

WRENCH:
We do know that we've given up our freedom for the sake of our health. Don't we want to see if we can have both?

TAB:
It's like you want to end up dead!

WRENCH:
Aren't you all desperate to see what the world outside looks like? Instead of relying on virtual communications and digital instruction? Looking at a screenshot of a sunset instead of an actual sunset? Pixilated seascapes instead of the ocean? We're relying on our dreams to see the sky, the trees —the grass!
What do you remember from before we came here?
Seriously. How much do you remember?

*No one replies. For, like, a long time.*

DEETS:
Books. Walls of books with multicolored spines.

GYM:
A cone of pink ice cream. Melting cold down my hand.

FLORA:
A glass case with a turtle eating lettuce.

TAB:
Guys. Those things are gone. Books and ice cream and turtles are gone.

BINS:
There's still lettuce.

WRENCH:
There will always be sky, Tab. There will always be clouds and stars—even if the radiation has messed up everything else.
Don't you want to see them again?

TAB:
Yes, but—

WRENCH:
What if these people—these voices—can help us see them? What if they can give us back the sky?

TAB:
In exchange for what, Wrench?

*WRENCH doesn't know how to answer.*

STEWARD:
The truth is, we don't even know that that's what they're promising.

WRENCH:
Steward—

STEWARD:

But
I think... we should find out.

TAB:

Seriously?

STEWARD:

I think we all need to see and hear on our own, don't you
Tab? We need to talk to these people and find out what they
want. Agreed?

*Pause.*

GYM:                              WRENCH:
Sure.                            Thank you, Stew.

TAB:                             FLORA:
You're out of your mind.         Yes. Yes please.

WRENCH:

And we shouldn't report it until we understand more.

STEWARD:

That's fair.

*Beat.*

Tailor?
You've been pretty quiet.
Do you think we should talk to them?

> *TAILOR turns off her VizCom. She turns away
> from the screen.*

She turned off her VizCom.

STEWARD (cont):
Why would she turn off her VizCom?

FLORA:
She's probably tired, Steward. She was up late, after all.

STEWARD:
Sure. Okay.
So, Wrench, Flora: How do we do this?

*WRENCH and FLORA exchange a look.*

*Blackout.*

*With a sudden explosion of music and light,
ASTRID STARPEPPER twinkles into existence.*

ASTRID STARPEPPER:
It's time time time, my happy Denizens, to learn your craft!
Everyone get their Hearpieces in! Vocational instruction will
begin in
Eight
Seven
Six
Five
Four
Three
Two
Have a great day of learning!

*Lights blink out on ASTRID and back up on the
DISC. The Denizens sit facing their respective
screens, but it's clear they are all on edge.
DEETS taps a pen nervously. FLORA pries the
dirt off the edge of a gardening tool. STEWARD
is trying hard to focus, but his brow is
furrowed. TAB is still furious. WRENCH doesn't*

*look at the screen, only polishes Johnny with a cloth. BINS is asleep. GYM keeps glancing towards the wall he shares with TAILOR. She has not moved from her bed from the previous scene.*

*GYM takes off his Hearpiece. He approaches the wall. He speaks in a whisper.*

### GYM:

Tailor?
Tailor, are you okay?

*She hears him, but doesn't reply.*

Tailor, you seemed really upset. It looked like you were pretty upset.
Are you doing your instruction?
Are you not talking because you're doing your instruction?
If you are, that's totally cool.
Or are you sick?
Tailor?

### TAILOR:

I'm not sick.

*GYM leans against the wall.*

### GYM:

Do you want to tell me what's going on?
You don't have to.
I know I'm probably not as, like, clever as Wrench or Steward. Or even Bins. But I'm here if you need to work things out. We used to do that a lot, right?

*Beat. Tailor says nothing.*

GYM (cont):

I wanted to tell you, I wasn't completely honest? When we were talking about dreams.

One time I had this dream that I was hiking up this mountain, like I was hiking up a trail up the side of this mountain, and I got to the top, and there was this beautiful skyline, you know? Bright pinks and oranges and yellows all winding into one another, braiding through each other with these streams of purple running through them, and then suddenly the stones beneath my foot gave way, and I started falling, falling through this chasm, this empty stony chasm and I was screaming, and the chasm had no end, and I fell and I fell and I fell, and all I could think about was the terror. But then I started thinking about it—inside the dream. Like, what was I finding so scary? Because it's not like there was ground coming up, or anything. I wasn't hurt—it was just falling forever, you know? Was I scared because I had no control? No control over my own body?

I thought, I'm going to take back my body, one muscle at a time. I'm going to regain control over this body. And you know what I started to do?

I started punching the air. I mean, it's a dream so I guess I didn't care about looking like a weirdo, but I started punching the air. And then kicking the air. And then head-butting the air as I fell, and for some reason—the laws of physics being whatever they want to be in dreams—I started slowing down. I started falling slower and slower and slower, punch after punch, kick after kick. Can you believe it?

Don't answer. That was rhetorical.

Or maybe not.

I was able to regain control. Within my own dream. I stopped falling. I started flying. And I flew all the way back, all the way back into that beautiful sky.

*GYM waits for a response; there is none.*

GYM (cont):
I was able to take back what the nightmare tried to take from me.
Tailor?
Are you there?

                    TAILOR:
I am.

                    GYM:
What do you think?
About the dream?

                    TAILOR:
I think it... helps.

                    GYM:
Cool.
That's cool.
Anyway, if you wanna talk, let me know.

                    TAILOR:
Thank you, Gym.

                    GYM:
You're welcome, Tailor.

            *They sit. Leaning against the wall.*

            *Lights shift, to WRENCH, in his cell. He is still
            polishing Johnny Rockets, but deep in thought.
            At last, a light bulb moment.*

WRENCH:
Elias.
Who is Elias?

*Wrench pulls off his Hearpiece and presses a button on the VizCom.*

Open private communication to Flora.

*Lights up on FLORA.*

Flora—

FLORA:
This is unbearable.
The waiting.

WRENCH:
All you do is wait.

FLORA:
Yes, but at the end of that waiting there are chives. There are radishes. At the end of this... who knows?

WRENCH:
Flora, who is Elias?

FLORA:
Beats me.

WRENCH:
The man said—in my not-so-dream, before the static and the sound went out—the man said as long as it takes until they can bring "Elias" home. Who is Elias?

FLORA:
I've never heard that name before.

WRENCH:
Do you think they believe Elias is in this DISC? They're looking for someone named Elias and they think he's in this DISC?

FLORA:
It's conceivable, I guess.

WRENCH:
Maybe it was someone who was here before we came. Maybe Elias is one of the previous Denizens.

FLORA:
How could we know without tapping into the system directly?

> *WRENCH presses another button on the VizCom.*

WRENCH:
Open a second private channel with Deets.

> *Lights come up on DEETS.*

Deets—

DEETS:
No.

WRENCH:
It's nothing big—

## DEETS:

I'm in the middle of my Vocational Instruction, and I don't have time to talk about the voices. I never heard them, I don't know them, and frankly, I'm a little frustrated you're trying to drag me into this mess.

## WRENCH:

Don't you want to—

## DEETS:

Let me stop you, Wrench. No. I don't want to. The only thing I want to do is stop writing, I want to stop writing for five minutes and let my hand rest because I think I'm getting carpal tunnel, and I don't understand why they refuse to give me a keyboard and let me type because I'm going through, like, four pens a week, Wrench. FOUR PENS A WEEK. Do you know how much ink that is?

## FLORA:

Deets, would you shut up and listen for a second?

## DEETS:

I will not shut up or listen.

## FLORA:

Deets—

## DEETS:

Helping you is dangerous, Flora.
When she punished you, it's because you made a choice. You made a choice and didn't take your meds and she caught you. I didn't make that choice. I got electrocuted with 250 volts and plunged in darkness and isolated from everyone because of what you did. Because of your choice.
I didn't deserve it.
Tailor doesn't deserve it either.
So you can figure this out yourself.

WRENCH:

No one deserves to get punished. We didn't do anything wrong.

DEETS:

That doesn't seem to matter to Miss She-of-the-neon-hairdos, Wrench. But because you two don't want to leave it alone, it's going to happen again. All of us are going to be punished. All of us.
I'm not going to help you.

FLORA:

I'm sorry.
I'm sorry that I got you in trouble. Both of you.
But you know why I decided to stop taking the... the you-know-whats?
I was giving up.

WRENCH:

Giving up?

FLORA:

Daring the sickness to come and get me.

WRENCH:

Why?

FLORA:

Because of this place! Because living here is barely a life. The same thing, every day, day after day, and we can't change it because we can't see each other. We can't talk to one another. I know it feels safe here, but this is not safety. This is torture. I hate it here so much. So I made a choice. Because something had to change and it was the only thing I had control over. My body. My medication.

DEETS:
Then why haven't you tried again?

FLORA:
Because of you, you idiot.
Because She told me that every night I threw away the... the
medicine, another one of you would be punished. Another
one of you would be tortured or electrocuted or starved. I felt
guilty. I still feel guilty.
But now... now I think there's a way out, Deets. There's a
path towards freedom—even if it's one I don't understand, I
truly believe it's there. I thought Tailor would be a good ally.
And I think you are, too.
Help us.
Please.

DEETS:
I can't.
There's no evidence it's real. The voices, the message, the
hope. It's a dream. It's a fantasy.
I deal in reality. You have no facts.

> DEETS is so sincere, FLORA is crushed. It's as
> though the air has been knocked out of her.

WRENCH:
Who's Elias?

> *Pause.*

DEETS:
Where did you hear that name?

WRENCH:
Do you know who that is?
Have you heard that name before?

*A siren starts to blare, and all of the lights in the cells are replaced by flashing red. A spotlight reveals ASTRID STARPEPPER, wearing her trademark smile, accompanied by a musical flourish.*

ASTRID STARPEPPER:
Bad bad bad news, Denizens! It looks like we've got a bio-radiation outbreak here in the DISC! Awwwwww. Which of you is it? It's not who you think! But before you collapse into a puddle of tears remember that there's always a sol sol solution!
Initiate Emergency Protocols!
This has been Astrid Starpepper!

*Musical flourish.*

Stay Say Say Safe, Everyone!

*ASTRID laughs as she fades from view, and the sirens go with her. The Denizens are left in a flashing red light.*

TAB:
Dammit!

FLORA:
Is everyone okay? Tailor?

TAILOR:
There's nothing—

STEWARD:
Everyone, check in. Wrench?

WRENCH:
I'm fine.

STEWARD:

Tab? Deets?


TAB:

Dammit!


STEWARD:

Calm down, Tab.


DEETS:

It's hard to see in this light.


BINS:

What's going on? Is it dinner?


FLORA:

The VizComs still work?


GYM:

What do we do?


STEWARD:

There are protocols in place for this.


TAB:

Who is it? Fess up!


STEWARD:

Tab! Protocols!


TAB:

Fine. I have instructions to distribute a supplement that will suppress the radiation sickness until we can get further medical attention.

STEWARD:
Wrench—send Johnny Rockets out.

>*WRENCH does so. Johnny stops by TAB's cell*
>*and retrieves the medication, distributing it to*
>*each Denizen. It's a small red pill.*

FLORA:
Steward, can you get the lights back on?

STEWARD:
I think so.

>*A few touches to the console, and STEWARD*
>*does so, although the red continues to flash.*
>*Their panic lessens.*

Does everyone have the supplement?

DEETS:
It's red.

WRENCH:
Steward—before we take this thing—

TAB:
It's medicine, Wrench.

WRENCH:
You need to know something.
The reason we could hear the voices—
We didn't take our meds.

TAB:
I knew it! I knew you were the one who is sick, and that's
why you were off-line!

WRENCH:
I was off-line because I was being punished by Astrid. I'm
not sick. There is nothing wrong with me.

STEWARD:
Why would taking our meds prevent us from hearing the
voices?

WRENCH:
The pills sedate us, knock us out at nights, just like they
caffeinate us in the mornings. The sedatives are so strong we
can't hear anything.

FLORA:
It's true.

BINS:
Yup.

TAB:
Does that mean none of you took your meds last night? Do
you know what an enormous health risk you pose right now?
Take your medicine before you kill yourselves!

TAILOR:
Tab—

TAB:
No stalling! Do it! I want to see each one of you swallow
these pills! One by one if I have to!

TAILOR:
Tab, when I talked to them—

TAB:
No more stupid excuses.

Deets. You first. Put the pill under your tongue. Do it so I can see it.

DEETS:

I... don't know...

TAB:

Do it!

*DEETS does so.*

Now swallow it.

*DEETS does so.*

Good. Bins? You're up. Put the pill under your tongue.

BINS:

I'm still supposed to be asleep? I got, like, a couple of hours left?

*DEETS clutches his stomach.*

TAB:

Put the pill in your mouth!

BINS:

Do we have water?

STEWARD:

Just swallow it dry, Bins.

> *The pain in DEETS' stomach becomes
> excruciating.  DEETS cries out, collapses.*

| GYM: | FLORA: |
|------|--------|
| What's that? | Deets, what's wrong? |

| WRENCH: | STEWARD: |
|---------|----------|
| Deets? | Say something!! Deets! |

*DEETS writhes around on the floor, muscles spasming.*

DEETS:
Oh god oh god oh god oh—

TAB:
What's happening?

WRENCH:
Bins! Get in there!

BINS:
It's not sanitary!

WRENCH:
Help her! Please! Get that pill out of her system!

*BINS, faster than we think possible of her, flings open the grate, and within seconds, she's inside DEETS' cell. She pulls her up from behind, and with a few well-placed thrusts of her fists into her stomach, DEETS begins to cough up the pill. BINS steps back as DEETS throws up onto the cell floor.*

*The Denizens stand in stunned silence.*

WRENCH:
Deets—are you okay?

*DEETS cries, coughing. The searing pain has stopped.*

BINS:
She's all right. I mean, she's a mess, but she's all right.

*BINS wrinkles her nose at the vomit.*

Do I have to clean this up?

FLORA:
*(near tears)* Oh, Deets. I'm so sorry. I'm so sorry.

TAB:
What... happened?

STEWARD:
She had a bad reaction.

GYM:
That's a bad reaction.

TAB:
I don't... I don't understand. Astrid said it was a supplement. What kind of supplement does that to a person?

TAILOR:
The kind that's not meant to work.

TAB:
What do you mean?

TAILOR:
The voice said:
There is no radiation.

TAB:

No radiation?

TAILOR:

It's all been a lie, Tab. The lessons. The tutorials. The
instruction. The documentary footage of people dying in the
streets. I told him that we didn't want to leave, that we were
protected from the bio-radiation as long as we remained in
the DISC, and he didn't know what I was talking about. He
said there wasn't a nuclear incident. He said there was no
uprising. No insurrection.
There is no radiation.

STEWARD:

Then why are we here?
What are we doing here?

WRENCH:

We won't know until we talk to him. Until we talk to the
voice tonight.

*TAB is left reeling by this.*

TAB:

I don't...

*DEETS coughs. BINS rubs DEETS' back.*

BINS:

You're gonna be okay, Deets.

*DEETS moans.*

I can get you a towel for the puke.

DEETS:

Thanks.

### TAB:

I don't get it.

### GYM:

Me neither.

### TAB:

Shut up.

### STEWARD:

Tab?

### TAB:

Just shut up. All of you. Shut up.
Do you have any idea how... hard it's been? Every day for eleven years? Listening to you going on about whatever stupid dreams and salads and how many freakin' pushups you can do in an hour—

### GYM:

It's a LOT.

### TAB:

SHUT UP.
Has it ever occurred to you that if I make one mistake, one tiny mistake, one of you dies? Can you imagine, for a moment, the sort of pressure that puts on me? Knowing that, at any minute, the medications could fail and one of you could die and then we all could die and I couldn't do anything about it? How am I supposed to fix that? I... I can't stop you from being sick, I can't stop you from not taking your medications—I can't do anything, but I'm expected to do everything.
You all suck for taking me for granted. You all... you all suck for making me responsible for your ingrateful frivolous existences.

TAB (cont):
And now we might not be sick at all. It might be some big
joke. It might be some giant lie. My whole purpose has
been...
I don't understand.

> *Beat.*

WRENCH:
None of us understand, Tab.
But we will soon enough.

> *Lights fade. Music, as we see time passing. Each*
> *Denizen in their cell, waiting for the Dark. No*
> *one speaks. No one does anything. They just sit,*
> *staring at the wall, waiting. Waiting. Finally,*
> *STEWARD speaks.*

STEWARD:
Wrench, send Johnny around.

> *JOHNNY makes the rounds, stopping by each*
> *delivery port. But no one reaches back to take*
> *anything from it. No one moves.*

Pills and water in everyone's delivery ports.
Everybody ready?
Thirty seconds to Dark.

> *They sit, silent and still for thirty seconds. No*
> *one moves.*

> *Blackout.*

> *The first light we see is the glowing golden eyes*
> *of Johnny Rockets. And then a voice cuts*
> *through the darkness.*

MAN:

Hello?
Tailor?
Anybody?

STEWARD:

We're here.

MAN:

You
You're here.
You're all here?
What—what's your name?

STEWARD:

My name is Steward. We're all here. We're waiting for you.

MAN:

Hello, Steward.
Forgive me, my heart is racing.
My name is Kent.

STEWARD:

Kent.

KENT:

I'd like to help get you out of the DISC, Steward.

STEWARD:

Why?
Why us?

KENT:

Because you don't belong in there. You belong out here. In the world.

STEWARD:

Kent: We were told that there is toxic radiation all over the country. We were told that we are in this DISC for protection. But you told Tailor that there is no radiation? That there never was a nuclear event that killed thousands of people?

KENT:

That's right. Is that what they told you?

TAB:

Who?
Is that what who told us?

KENT:

The Department of Security.

DEETS:

The Department of Security?

KENT:

Yes.
The DISC isn't a health facility.
It's a prison.

STEWARD:

But... we haven't done anything wrong.

KENT:

We know.

GYM:

What about the other DISCs? Huh? Are those prisons, too?

KENT:

There aren't any others.

WRENCH:

What?

KENT:

There was a rising political movement. People were standing against government hypocrisy and inequality. Passionate, vocal critics threatened systems that had been in place for hundreds of years. When the minds of the people began to shift, the government realized they couldn't detain these critics without a blowback from the larger population. It would have turned them all into martyrs.
So they took all of you instead.

FLORA:

They... took us?

KENT:

You were kidnapped from your homes and put there. To ensure their silence.

TAILOR:

Our parents.

KENT:

The government promised your safety on the condition that the activism stopped. A few of us fled the country. Some of us are in hiding, but they wouldn't dare speak out for fear something might happen to you.

FLORA:

Something did happen to us.

KENT:

We know.

FLORA:

We don't deserve to be here.

GYM:

What sort of a country does that? What sort of country takes kids from their families and locks them up?

KENT:

This one.
But we can get you out.

BINS:

Now?

KENT:

Yes.

TAB:

Why now? We've been here for nearly twelve years. We've been alone, and you've done nothing.

KENT:

We've been trying to reach you that whole time, I swear.

TAB:

You should have TRIED HARDER.

KENT:

We did, I promise you—
But every time we made any progress, they threatened to hurt one of you. Or all of you. That's why we need to get you out.

WRENCH:

Why do you care so much what happens to us?

*There is a pause.*

It's Elias, isn't it?

KENT:

Yes.

WRENCH:

Elias is your son.

KENT:

Yes.

WRENCH:

You think he's one of us?

*Beat.*

DEETS:

We all had other names.
Elias.
Thomas.
Lily.
Marcus.
Sarah.
India.
Kristin.
My name is Allison. I wrote them all down.
In case... in case.

FLORA:

Oh, Deets.

DEETS:

You grow stuff, Flora; I know stuff.

> *A moment in which everyone contemplates the
> life they never led.*

WRENCH:
So what do we have to do? To get out?


KENT:
We installed an emergency release.
All of you have to do is pull it—together.
Reach out your hands towards—

> *The sudden blast of sound, and ASTRID
> STARPEPPER appears, cradling a baseball bat
> in her dainty hands. With a shout, she brings it
> down on Johnny Rockets, again and again and
> again, until she smashes the little robot to
> pieces. The transmission from KENT is gone.*
>
> *ASTRID looks up from the wreckage and
> addresses them.*

ASTRID STARPEPPER:
Good good good evening, everyone. I'm sorry to say we've
had some technical difficulties with our Johnny Rockets, and
therefore will not be ay ay able to assist you further until a
new one is manufactured.  We apologize for the in in
inconvenience.

> *The Denizens protest again.*

There will also be an inexplicable power outage in
eight
seven
six
five
now.

> *The lights go out in the entire DISC. Only
> ASTRID remains illuminated.*

ASTRID STARPEPPER (cont):

It will be Dark now, I'm afraid. For as long as we deem
appropriate.

WRENCH:

You can't keep us here forever!

ASTRID STARPEPPER:

We shall see, won't we?
This is Astrid Starpepper—

*A musical flourish.*

Stay Safe, Everyone.

*ASTRID blips out. The stage is left in darkness.*

TAB:

What do we do? Steward?

STEWARD:

I don't know.

GYM:

We're gonna die in the darkness.

WRENCH:

We're not going to die.
The man, Kent—he said to reach towards the sound of his
voice.
There must be a switch of some kind.

STEWARD:

His voice came from Johnny Rockets. We can't all reach
Johnny Rockets.

BINS:

What's left of Johnny Rockets.

*Beat.*

DEETS:

The delivery ports.

TAILOR:

The delivery ports?

DEETS:

We should reach our hands through the delivery ports.

FLORA:

Or on the other side?

DEETS:

Yes.

STEWARD:

Did you know about--?

DEETS:

Just a guess.

WRENCH:

Everyone, reach through—

*They do so, in the darkness.*

GYM:

I think I feel something—

TAB:

A switch—there's some sort of switch—

BINS:

Here, too.

FLORA:

Pull it!

STEWARD:

Wait!

WRENCH:

Steward?

STEWARD:

Be sure, everyone.
Before we do this.
Be sure.
Because we don't know what happens next. If the world
we're about to see will be the one we see in our dreams, or
our nightmares. So, I just want us to... be sure.
We have a choice.
We are making a choice. To no longer be safe. In the world.

*Beat.*

Eight
Seven
Six
Five
Four
Three
Two
One

> *They all press the 'switch' simultaneously, and*
> *as they do, there is a hiss, a blast of fog, and the*
> *walls of the D.I.S.C. begin to rise away, rise into*
> *the air. And as they do, light begins to come onto*

*the stage—the Denizens look at one another.
They have never seen each other before. But as
the walls continue, the stage is filled with light.
It is a sunrise. It is their first sunrise, all around
them, and each of the Denizens turn out to see it.*

*One by one, they reach out, and take the hands
of the person beside them, still looking out at the
world. There is wind. There are birds. There is
music.*

### BINS:

The trees.

### GYM:

The grass.

### FLORA:

The sky.

### TAILOR:

It's all there.

### TAB:

It's all still there.

### DEETS:

It's like a dream.

### WRENCH:

No.
Not like a dream.

*They bask in the world.
Lights fade to black.*

### END OF PLAY